All About Sound

by Kirsten Anderson

What is sound?

Stop and listen. What do you hear?
Maybe you hear voices. Maybe you
hear cars. Maybe you hear birds singing.
You might even hear music playing.

Those are all different sounds. Sound is made when an object vibrates. **Vibrate** means to move quickly back and forth.

When you sing, parts of your throat vibrate.
Put your fingers on the front of your throat
and talk. Do you feel the buzz under your fingers?
Those are your vocal cords vibrating.

A guitar has strings. When the strings vibrate, they make sound. You can see the guitar strings in this picture.

Loudness

Sounds are not all the same. They are different in some ways. **Loudness** is one way to explain different sounds. Sound can be loud or soft.

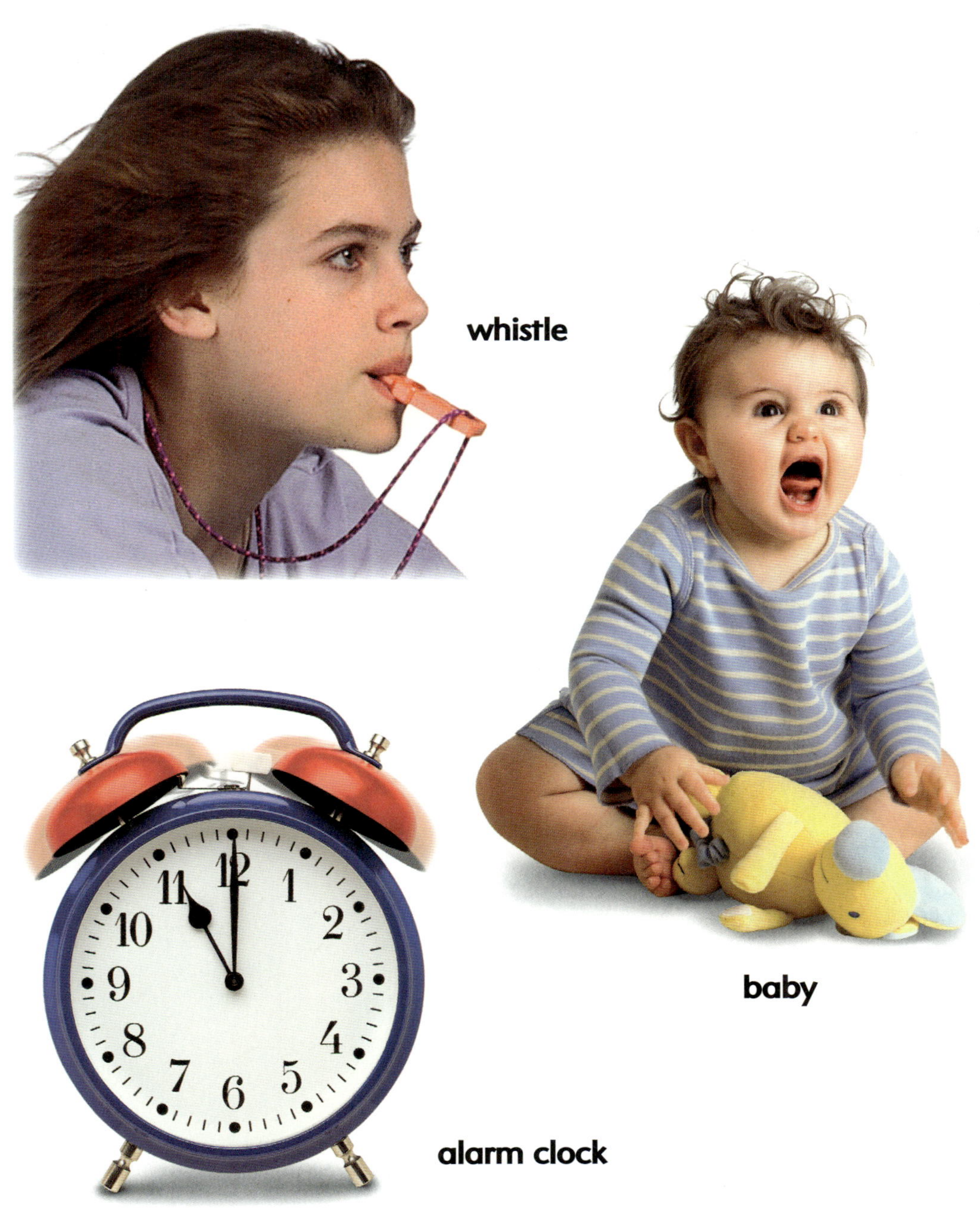

Sound can be loud. Look at the pictures. These things make loud sounds. You can make a loud sound when you shout.

Sound can be soft. The things in these pictures make soft sounds. You can make a soft sound when you whisper.

Pitch

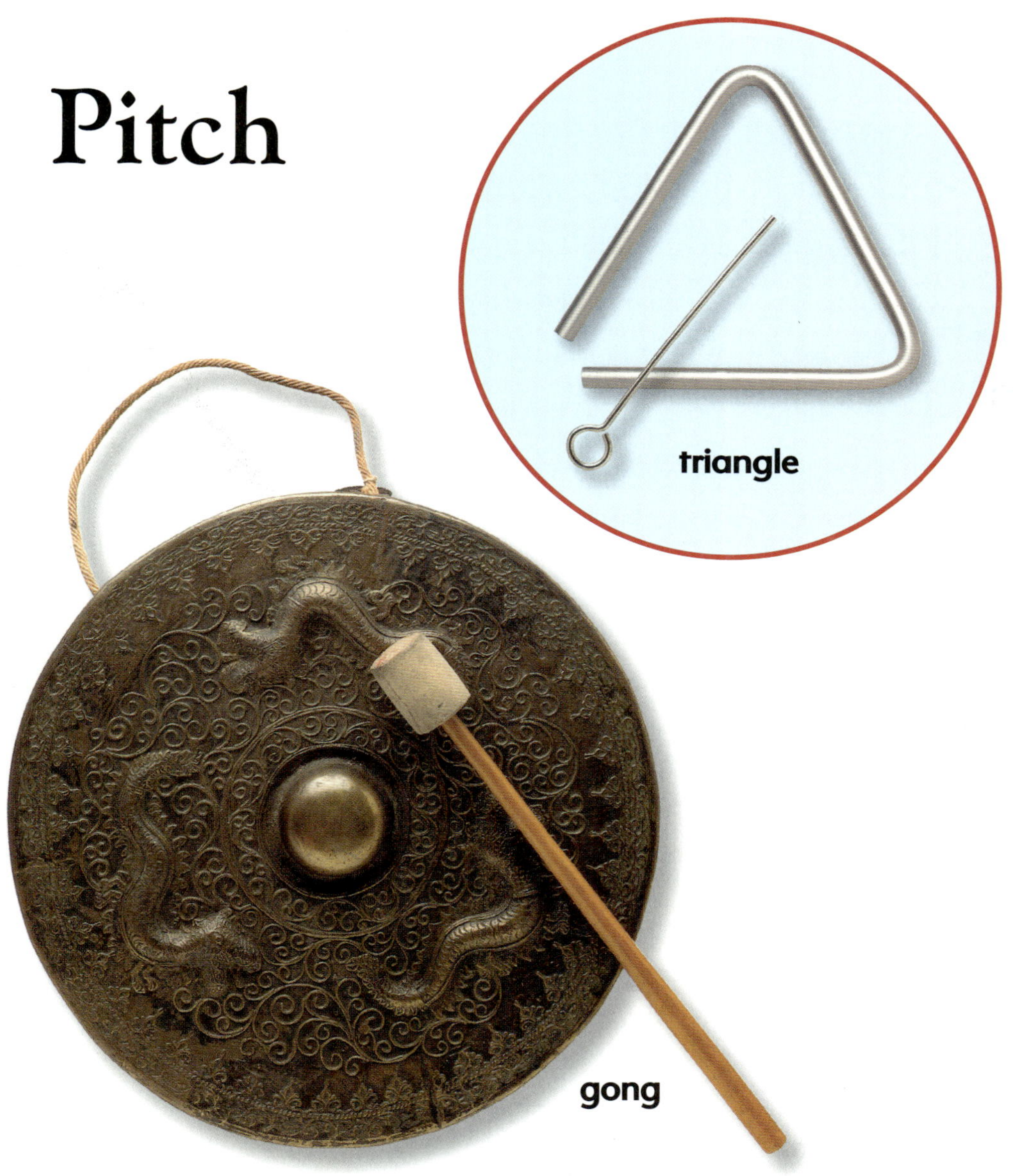

Pitch is another way to explain sound. Pitch can be high or low. Objects that vibrate quickly make a high-pitched sound. Objects that vibrate slowly make a low-pitched sound.

You can use bottles filled with water to make high-pitched or low-pitched sounds. Fill some bottles with a lot of water. Fill some bottles with a little water.

Blow over the tops of the bottles. This makes the air inside the bottles vibrate. The bottles with a lot of air will make a low-pitched sound. The bottles with a little air will make a high-pitched sound.

Blow over the tops of bottles of water. The bottles will make different sounds.

10

Animals make sounds with different pitches. A lion's roar has a low pitch. A cat's meow has a high pitch.

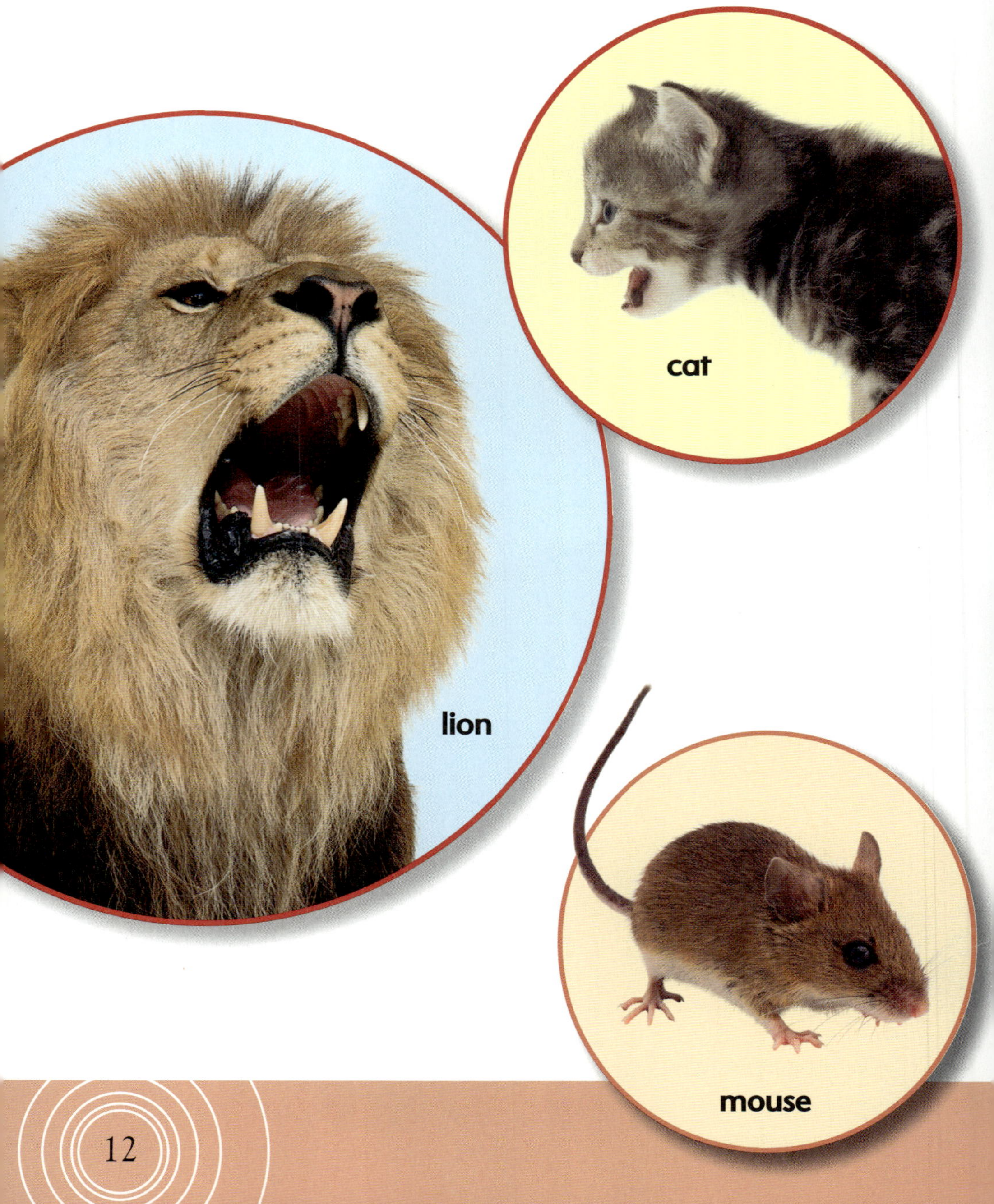

Look at the pictures. Which ones show
high-pitched sounds? Which ones show
low-pitched sounds?

Sound Travels

Sound can move through gases, liquids, and solids.

Sound travels through gases. Air is a gas.

Look at the picture of the roller coaster.
The riders are shouting.

The other people in the park can hear them.
They can hear them because sound travels through air.

Water is a liquid. Sound can travel through liquids. Sound travels faster through liquids than through gases. Sound travels faster through water than through air.

Whales make sounds. Their sounds travel through water. Other whales can hear these sounds many miles away.

Sound travels through solids. Sound travels faster through solids than through either gases or liquids.

A string is a solid. Sound can travel through string.

Take two cups. Tie them together with a long piece of string. Stand in one room with one cup. Send a friend to another room with the other cup. Pull the string tight. Speak into the cup. Your friend will quickly hear your voice.

Animal Sounds

Animals make sounds using parts of their bodies. Cicadas vibrate small parts of their bellies. This works like tiny drums.

Elephants blow air through their trunks. Their trunks vibrate. This works like playing a bugle.

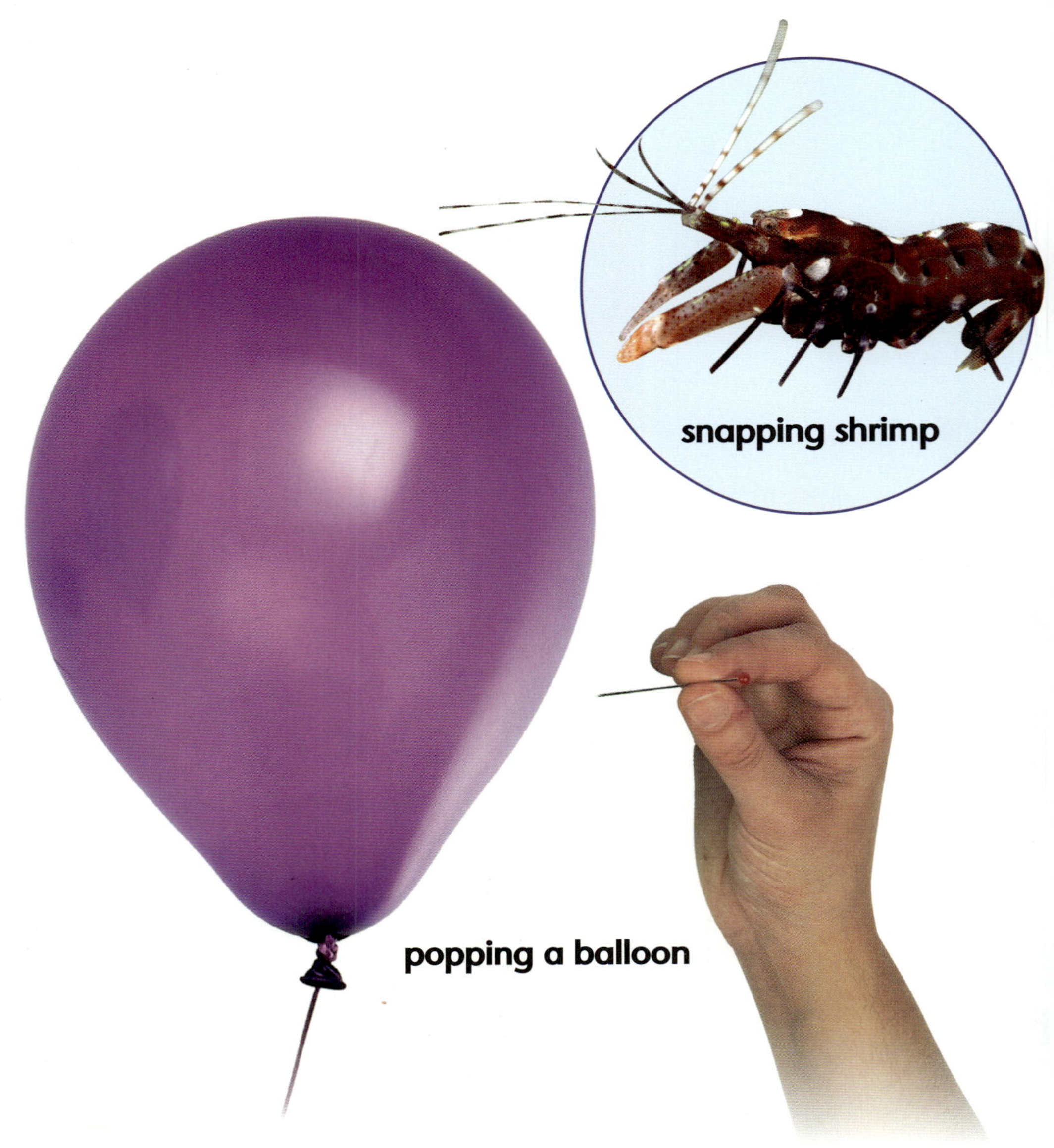

snapping shrimp

popping a balloon

Snapping shrimp make sounds with their large claws. The shrimp open and close their claws fast. They catch air bubbles in their claws. Then the bubbles pop. This works like popping a balloon.

Sound Is All Around You

Now you know how sound is made. Sound can be loud or soft. Sound can be high pitched or low pitched. Sound can travel fast or slow.

Next time you are outside, listen to the sounds around you. The world is full of sound!

Glossary

loudness how loud or quiet a sound is

pitch how low or high a sound is

vibrate to move quickly back and forth